Count The
Tractors!

This Book Belongs To:

_____

Your child loves farm tractors?

At the end of the book, please find our e-mail address to send us an e-mail, and we will send you completely free farm tractor coloring pages, that every toddler would be sure to enjoy! Simply write "Yes, I want to receive free farm tractor coloring pages!" and we will send them to you, completely for free! The coloring pages are in printable PDF format.

Copyright © By: Jasper Daesdonk Publishing

Count all the tractors like this one! ➡️

Congratulations! You guessed correctly

There were 3 such tractors in the picture

Count all the tractors like this one!

Congratulations! You guessed correctly

There were 5 such tractors in the picture

Find 2 of the same tractors!

Congratulations! You guessed correctly

Here are 2 of the same tractors

Count all the tractors like this one!

Congratulations! You guessed correctly

There were 2 such tractors in the picture

Are there more of these ![orange tractor with trailer] or these ![teal tractor] tractors?

Congratulations! You guessed correctly

There were more of these

 x4

 x3

Count all the tractors like this one!

Congratulations! You guessed correctly

There was 1 such tractor in the picture

Count all the tractors like this one! →

Congratulations! You guessed correctly

There were 4 such tractors in the picture

Count how many of the same tractors are on this page!

Congratulations! You guessed correctly

There were 5 of the same tractors on that page

Count all the tractors like this one!

Congratulations! You guessed correctly

There were 6 such tractors in the picture

Count all the tractors like this one! ➡️

Congratulations! You guessed correctly

There were 2 such tractors in the picture

Are there more of these 🚜 or these 🚜 tractors?

Congratulations! You guessed correctly

There were more of these

x2

x1

Count all the tractors like this one! ⟹

Congratulations! You guessed correctly

There were 8 such tractors in the picture

Count all the tractors like this one!

Congratulations! You guessed correctly

There was 1 such tractor in the picture

Count all the tractors like this one!

Congratulations! You guessed correctly

There were 3 such tractors in the picture

Find 2 of the same tractors!

Congratulations! You guessed correctly

Here are 2 of the same tractors

Count all the tractors like this one!

Congratulations! You guessed correctly

There were 7 such tractors in the picture

Count all the tractors like this one!

Congratulations! You guessed correctly

There were 4 such tractors in the picture

Are there more of these  or these  tractors?

Congratulations! You guessed correctly

There were more of these

 x5

x2

Count all the tractors like this one!

Congratulations! You guessed correctly

There were 10 such tractors in the picture

I AM VERY GRATEFUL YOU PURCHASED THIS BOOK. I HOPE YOU AND YOUR CHILD SPEND AN UNFORGETTABLE TIME HAVING FUN AND LEARNING TOGETHER FROM THIS BOOK.

IF YOU CAN, I WOULD BE EXTREMELY GRATEFUL IF YOU COULD LEAVE A REVIEW ON AMAZON. WE ARE A SMALL FAMILY BUSINESS AND DEPEND ON REVIEWS TO REACH MORE FAMILIES.

THANK YOU AGAIN FOR YOUR PURCHASE AND YOUR TRUST. I HOPE YOU ENJOY YOUR BOOK AND HAVE A GREAT TIME WITH YOUR FAMILY

HAVE A NICE DAY!

WE HOPE THE BOOK HAS MET YOUR EXPECTATIONS. IF YOU FOUND ANY MISTAKES IN THE BOOK, PLEASE CONTACT US BY EMAIL, AND WE WILL CORRECT THEM AS SOON AS POSSIBLE

office.dannyd@gmail.com

INDEPENDENTLY PUBLISHED

Jasper Daesdonk Publishing

Made in the USA
Columbia, SC
05 December 2022

72595236R00024